Faces

A person's face tells us more about its owner than any other part of the body. It shows what mood someone is in, how old they are, and a good deal about their character. It is not surprising, then, that artists interested in people should often choose to concentrate on their faces.

Some of the pictures in this book are by great portraitists whose aim has been to capture as good a likeness as possible, but these are placed alongside masks from primitive cultures, paintings of hideous monsters, cruel caricatures and faces remoulded by the vivid imaginations of modern artists. The result is a strikingly varied portrait gallery.

At the back are some facts about the artists in the book as well as some ideas for finding out more about pictures.

Giles Waterfield is Director of Dulwich Picture Gallery, and teaches History of Art at Alleyn's School, Dulwich College and James Allen's Girls' School, London.

Ronald Parkinson is Head of Education at the Victoria and Albert Museum, London.

LOOKING AT ART

Faces

Giles Waterfield

Consultant Editor: Ronald Parkinson
Head of Education, Victoria and Albert Museum, London

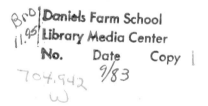
A MARGARET K. McELDERRY BOOK

Atheneum   1982   New York

Jacket Giuseppe Arcimboldo, *Summer,* 1563 (detail). Full picture reproduced on p. 14.

Frontispiece Mask of the Iroquois Indians. Full picture reproduced on p.36.

LIBRARY OF CONGRESS CATALOGING IN PUBLICATION DATA
Waterfield, Giles.
    Faces.

    (Looking at art)
    "A Margaret K. McElderry Book."
    SUMMARY: Discussions accompany an assortment of
portraits from many periods and countries.
    1. Portraits—Juvenile literature.   2. Face in art—
Juvenile literature.   3. Painting—Juvenile literature.
[1. Portraits.   2. Face in art.   3. Painting—History]
I. Parkinson, Ronald.   II. Title.   III. Series.
ND1300.W38   757   82-3935
ISBN 0-689-50251-6   AACR2

Copyright © 1982 by Wayland Publishers Ltd.
All rights reserved
Printed in Italy by
G. Canale & C.S. p.A., Turin
First American Edition

Contents

Looking at Art

Art is for everyone. With the help of a selection of
outstanding pictures, combined with lively,
down-to-earth discussion, this series shows
clearly how rewarding it is to understand and
enjoy paintings. Each book takes a theme, looks
at the way it has been treated by famous artists
from many different countries throughout the
ages, and compares in simple language their
varied styles and ideas.

Faces
People at Home
People at Work

List of Plates

Profile on royalty

Antonio
Pisanello, *Este
Princess,*
c.1430.

8

Lost princess

The two ladies on this page both belonged to royal families, one in Italy and the other in England, but about four hundred years apart. Pisanello's portrait was lost for a long time, and during those years people forgot the lady's name. We do know, though, that she was a princess, and that she belonged to an Italian family called d'Este. We can tell this from her sleeve, which is embroidered with a two-handled vase, the sign of the d'Estes. From the flowers in the background, we may guess that this picture was painted at the time of her marriage.

The stamp of approval

We know the name of the other lady: Queen Victoria, who reigned over England for most of the nineteenth century. This is not a portrait, but a postage stamp. It was a very special stamp: the first one regularly sold in England.

Postage within England then cost one old penny (less than a ½p nowadays) and so it is called the 'Penny Black'. At the time, Victoria was a young girl: she is shown with her hair in a bun, wearing a little crown (or tiara), and looking straight ahead. Only her head and neck can be seen, and her expression is more severe than the d'Este Princess's. Victoria's face is an offical one, for public occasions.

An official view

Although these two heads are quite different, in one way they are the same. Each is shown from the side, in what is called profile. If you try it yourself, you will find that drawing someone's head in outline is one of the easiest ways of catching a likeness. But these ladies were not shown in profile to save trouble. When it was decided to show Queen Victoria's head from the side on this stamp, an old tradition was being used, found especially on coins and medals. Pisanello also designed medals, which may explain why he shows the d'Este Princess in profile. If you look at a modern coin or postage stamp you will see that the idea is much the same.

Why do you think profiles are so suitable for official views of kings and queens? Partly because the lines are easily reproduced in metal, but also because the outline makes a strong picture which can easily be remembered and because the sitter looks serious and dignified. Victoria was only about twenty in 1840, and her face then was pretty rather than impressive, but in the stamp she looks as imposing as a Roman empress.

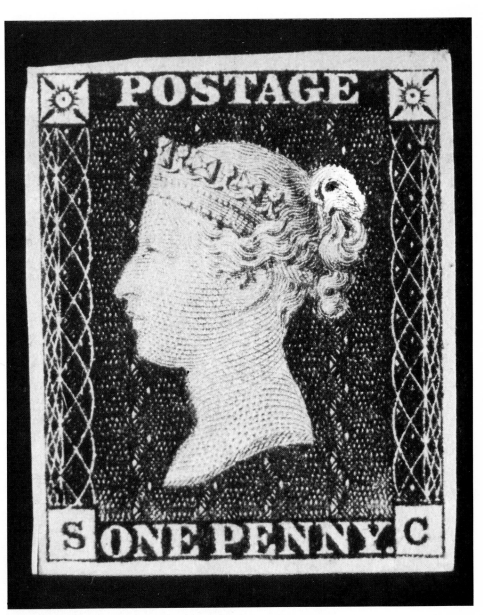

The Penny Black, the first stamp regularly sold in England.

Elder statesmen

Dressed for the part

Although one of these portraits is three hundred years older than the other, they have a good deal in common. Both show men in public life, of the same age, seen with their heads turned slightly away from the spectator, a position which makes a portrait less dominating than a full-face, but more personal than a profile. The artists' approaches to their sitters, however, are quite different.

The man with the strange hat is Leonardo Loredan, who was painted in 1501 when he was about sixty-five. Loredan had recently become the Doge (or Duke) of Venice, then an important independent state. He wears a skull-cap, the Doge's traditional head-gear, and magnificent silk robes. This picture is meant to show the stateliness of his position. George Washington was also an important public figure. In 1796, when this portrait was painted by the American artist, Gilbert Stuart, he was sixty-four and was President of the United States. Eighteenth-century America was a less formal place than Venice. Washington is not shown in state dress: he wears a black velvet coat and white ruffles, like any gentleman of the time.

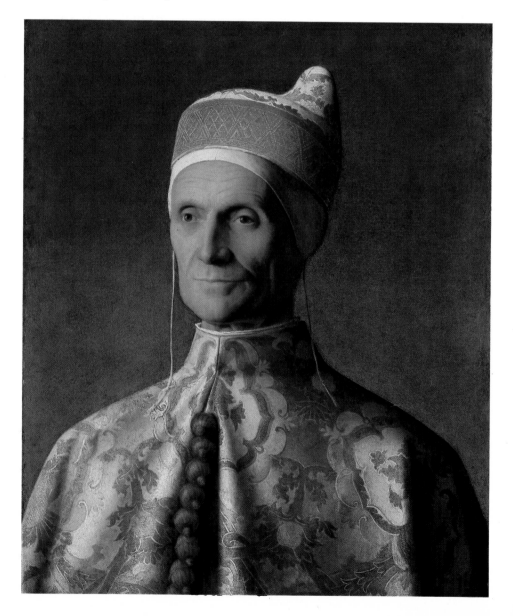

Giovanni Bellini, *Doge Loredan*, 1501.

Gilbert Stuart, *George Washington*, 1796.

Eyes on the move

Do you think that the faces of these two men are alike? Both have a look of authority, expressed in their serious gaze, and in their firm, thin, unsmiling mouths. But their eyes are quite different. The eye is perhaps the most expressive and revealing part of the face. When you are talking to someone, it is the eyes you look at. Unlike Loredan, who is looking away from the spectator, Washington stares straight at him. People often say of a portrait that 'the eyes follow you round the room'. They do in Washington's portrait. Inspect this picture, and any others in the book with eyes that seem to look at you: can you see how the artist achieves this effect? It is by putting the eyeballs in the very middle of the eye.

Involving the onlooker?

The mood of the two pictures is different too. In the portrait of the Doge there is no movement; he looks remote and timeless, like a piece of sculpture. With Washington, we know more about the conditions in which the picture was painted. By 1796, he was so tired of having his portrait painted that the artist had to tell amusing stories to stop a 'most appalling vacuity' from 'spreading over his countenance', and the uncomfortable look round his mouth was caused by his new false teeth. With him there is much more feeling of the moment when the portrait was painted, and of a connection between him and the spectator.

Re-making faces

An initiation mask from Zaire, Africa.

It doesn't look human!

So far all the faces you have seen have been recognizable views of people as you expect to see them. Here is something different. One of these faces is a carved wooden mask from Africa; we do not know exactly when it was made, or by whom. The other is a painting by one of the most famous artists of the twentieth century, Picasso. Though the purpose of these two works is not the same, the approach has something in common. The two artists are not interested in showing faces 'realistically' — that is, as people usually look. Instead, they are reinterpreting faces, making something new out of the features (eyes and nose and mouth) for a particular reason. No woman ever had hair the colour of Picasso's weeping woman's, or such eyes; and it is hard to know whether the mask shows a human being or an animal. But the impact that each makes is strong.

A mask with strange powers

The mask comes from Zaire. It belonged to the Songe tribe, and had a particular purpose: it was used in initiation. Every boy at a certain age moved from childhood to adulthood, and this event was marked by special ceremonies. These often included dances, in which the people initiating the children would be disguised in raffia cloaks and masks. These masks were precious and magical; it was thought that they were the incarnations of the magic spirits and dead heroes of the tribe, and so the masks were not made to look like humans. You can see that from the one here, with the ridge on the top of the head, the enormous hooded eyes and flat nose, and snout-like mouth.

Weeping picture

Picasso, who was Spanish, was one of the first Western artists to take an interest in African art, and it very much influenced his own. He learnt from what was called 'primitive art' that it was not necessary to paint people according to the old rules, but that an artist could often express his feelings more powerfully by distorting his sitter's face. Here he paints a woman (in fact a friend of his) dressed in ordinary clothes. As the title suggests, the point of this picture is to indicate the emotion she is suffering. Everything contributes: her crumpled face, her twisted mouth and agonized eyes, the tension in her fingers, the strange colouring. Though the picture may not be 'like' the woman, it *is* like a woman weeping.

Pablo Picasso, *Woman Weeping*, 1937.

13

No people are recognizable in the pictures on this page. These faces are not taken from ordinary experience, but from the imagination of the artists. The faces they paint are created by turning one thing into another; theirs is a kind of magic painting.

A disturbing harvest

The head on the left was painted in 1563 by Giuseppe Arcimboldo, as you can see from the writing on its neck and shoulders. What *is* this thing? If you look at it from a distance it may appear to be a man's head, with a headdress. But not

close to. This picture represents *Summer*, and everything in it is a product of the summer harvest: fruit and vegetables for the face, flowers and grain for the hair, and a coat of wheat. It is not very pleasant to look at; it is as if the skin had been stripped off the face, leaving a strange structure underneath. It

Giuseppe Arcimboldo, *Summer*, 1563.

Salvador Dali, *Apparition of a Face and a Fruit-dish on a Beach,* 1938.

looks rather like a picture from an anatomy book, designed to show how the human body is put together. Arcimboldo was painting for the Emperors of Austria and their courts, and pictures like this were no doubt meant to amuse; but don't you think that it is disturbing and frightening as well?

Fantasy from another world

The other picture is certainly meant to disturb you. What do you see at first? Probably a beach at the front of the picture, with rocks behind, and the sea in the distance; and on the right a bridge over a lake, and a field twisting away into some black mountains. But other things appear in this picture: 'apparitions'. The picture is called *Apparition of a Face and Fruit-dish on a Beach'*. The fruit-dish is in the middle and the face glowers out of the sand. And on the right, what about that landscape? Look at the bridge and the water, and the field leading to the mountain. Don't they turn into something else too?

Super-real

Salvador Dali, who painted this picture, was interested in 'Surrealism', which means anything beyond 'the real', such as you might see in dreams, or in your mind. He especially liked anything that changes its appearance as you stare at it.

15

Born to be king

PARVVLE PATRISSA, PATRIÆ VIRTVTIS ET HÆRES
ESTO, NIHIL MAIVS MAXIMVS ORBIS HABET.
GNATVM VIX POSSVNT COELVM ET NATVRA DEDISSE,
HVIVS QVEM PATRIS, VICTVS HONORET HONOS.
ÆQVATO TANTVM, TANTI TV FACTA PARENTIS,
VOTA HOMINVM, VIX QVO PROGREDIANTVR, HABENT
VINCITO, VICISTI. QVOT REGES PRISCVS ADORAT
ORBIS, NEC TE QVI VINCERE POSSIT, ERIT.

An important baby

These pictures show the same person: Edward VI, King of England from 1547 to 1553. Although he only lived to be fifteen, he was often painted because he was the only son of the King. In these paintings he is seen full-face and rather oddly in profile.

The full-face portrait was done in 1539, when the Prince was less than two years old. It was presented to his father, on New Year's Day, by the painter, and the King was so pleased that he gave Holbein a large gilt cup. Why do you think the King liked the painting so much?

Wise beyond his years

Remember that Edward was still really a baby, as his face shows: he has no lines on his fat, smooth cheeks or his high forehead, and his eyes stare forward. At the same time, this is obviously not an ordinary boy. He is splendidly dressed, with his feathered hat, his velvet clothes, and the chain round his neck. His hands, too, are important: one holds a rattle, but with dignity (just as, when he is older, he will grasp the sceptre), and the other is raised as though saluting the spectator.

But it is his face that is most interesting. Holbein has made it large and solid, so that you can almost feel the flesh. He has done

this partly by drawing a firm outline to the face, which ends in the Prince's little chin; and partly by highlighting and shading. Look at the light on the forehead, the chin and the cheeks, and at how carefully this contrasts with the shadows. And what about the Prince's expression? We know he is very young, but we can tell that this child is destined to be somebody special.

Artistic tricks

The other portrait is a surprise. It was painted when Edward was nine years old, as you can see from the Latin: 'Aetatis Svae 9'. 'EP' stands for 'Eduardus Princeps — Edward the Prince'. You can of course see *two* pictures; but these are photographs of the same piece of wood on which the picture was painted. This is what is called an 'anamorphic' portrait, one painted deliberately as a distortion. From the front it looks peculiar, with the Prince's nose very long and his face very flat; but viewed from the side or through a special contraption, it turns into an ordinary profile. This painting was extremely popular at Court, and was kept on a stand in the King's palace at Whitehall, with a viewing machine in front of it. Can you see any ways in which Scrots' Edward looks like the Edward in Holbein's portrait?

Guillim Scrots, *Edward VI — anamorphic portrait*, 1546.

17

(Left) Hans Holbein, *Edward VI as a Child,* 1539.

Two heads, six faces

Study for a sculpture

Charles I, King of England from 1625 to 1649, was very interested in art, and brought many painters to his Court including the great portraitist, Anthony Van Dyck. Van Dyck often painted the King. In this triple portrait, he shows the King full-face, and in profile, and turned half away from the spectator. It was done for a purpose: a sculpture was to be made of the King by the Italian, Bernini. Bernini lived in Rome, so this portrait was specially made for him to work from, and was sent out to him in Italy.

The 'Van Dyck face'

We know that Charles I looked more or less like this; what we might not guess is that he was small, and nervous-looking. The artist has created what is now called a 'Van Dyck' face: an oval outline with a high forehead and long, curling hair, large sad eyes under dark eyebrows, and a mouth almost disappearing between the bushy moustache and the thin, pointed beard. Compare the three views of the King. They are linked by his dignified expression, his air of melancholy, and his elegant manner.

The all-seeing face

Our second triple face has another purpose. It is a mask, and comes from the Ekpo society of the Ekoi tribe, in Nigeria. The Ekpo is a secret society, concentrating on punishing offenders. While carrying out their duties, its members wear large helmet-masks like this one. This mask is made of wood, covered with antelope skin; the eyes are inlaid with tin, the hair is of wooden pegs and the teeth are sticks. Above are two twisted antelope horns. The light-coloured open eyes mean that this is a female mask. The round marks on the side of the face showed the wearer's rank in society.

A disturbing power

Can you see any likenesses between the two triple faces? The style of looks is quite different (compare the eyebrows, the noses, the mouths) and so were their purposes. Unlike the pictures of Charles I, the mask has a symbolic importance, a meaning behind what you see. The faces look in all directions, showing that the spirit which the masks represent controls the past and the future, and understands everything. Though these objects are so unalike, they both have a disturbing quality, and suggest how powerful a head can be when you see it from several angles.

(Left) Sir Anthony Van Dyck, *Charles I in Three Positions,* 1637.

(Right) A three-faced mask from the Ekoi tribe, only two faces visible.

19

What is beauty?

So far we have not thought much about beauty and ugliness in faces. Ideas of what is handsome or attractive vary a great deal in different societies and generations. Here are two rather special examples: the heads of two gods, which have survived for hundreds of years, one from Greece and one from Central America. Both of these gods are shown as young men, and both represent what in each society was considered ideal beauty.

A Greek god. . .

Look first at Hermes. In ancient Greece, Hermes (known to the Romans as Mercury) was the god of commerce, wrestling and everything that required skill; as the messenger of his father Jupiter, he wore winged sandals. This statue was carved for a temple in Olympia, in eastern Greece, by one of the greatest Greek sculptors, Praxiteles. It shows Hermes carrying on one arm his little half-brother Dionysus, who was to become god of wine. Hermes has the features that the ancient Greeks most admired. His eyes are set wide apart, the nose is long and straight, the mouth perfectly regular; his face is oval, and he wears his hair short. Since this is a sculpture, we can also admire his fine profile. He seems extremely handsome to us today, because Western ideas of good looks — particularly in men — are very much influenced by what was admired more than 2,000 years ago in Greece.

Praxiteles, *Hermes*, c. 350 B.C.

. . .And a Central American God

Compare Hermes with the god of Maize. (Maize was one of the basic foods of the people who worshipped him.) This is a stone head belonging to the Maya people of Honduras, Central America. The head dates from about A.D. 750, and came from high on the outer wall of an immense temple, now a ruin. This, too, represents a society's idea of perfect beauty. It is not like the Greek one: the forehead is much flatter under the great headdress, the nose wider, the eyes large and set close together, and the lips fuller and inclined to stick out. It is a strong, peaceful face and we can see why the Maya people so admired it.

The god of Maize, Honduras, Central America.

A special quality

Of course, statues or paintings of gods must have a particular quality. They are not likely to be shown as angry, or worried, or grinning, but as remote and calm. Try to remember a painting of Jesus Christ that you may have seen. Do you think his face resembles these two gods in any way?

21

Here we have two princesses. No one is sure who the lady in the white headdress is, but she is probably Marie de Valengin, the daughter of the Duke of Burgundy in the fifteenth century. The other person is a queen. She was Marianna, the daughter of the Emperor of Germany, and was born in Vienna in 1634, and later became Queen of Spain. At the time of her wedding she was only fifteen, and this portrait was made two years afterwards by Velasquez, the King's painter.

As pretty as a princess?

Since both of these ladies were royal and rich, as well as young, you might expect that the artists would show them as beautiful, however they looked in reality. Do you think they are? If you do not, remember that at the time they were painted, faces like these may have been more admired than they are now. Fashions of the time, like ways of arranging hair, had an effect on their appearance. Marie de Valengin wears an unusual small hat, with a white veil over her head and hanging down behind. Her hair is scraped back to make her forehead seem as high as possible. Marianna's hairstyle, to our eyes, is extraordinary. Her hair is arranged so that it sticks out spectacularly on either side of her face, and is decorated with ribbons and a headdress.

The royal burden

Whereas in van der Weyden's *Lady*, the most important part of the picture is the face, the painting of *Marianna* is a full-length portrait

(one which shows a person from head to foot). In a 'full-length', the sitter's face can be very important, and so in a way it is here; but it has to compete with the hair, the curtains beside the figure, the enormous skirt and the handkerchief. Do you think that the way that this little queen's face is almost swallowed up by all these other things tell us something about the life Marianna had to lead?

A puzzling character

Now look again at Marie de Valengin. At first the way she is painted — her hair for example — makes her seem remote, almost like a nun. But although her eyes are calm they are full of thought; her mouth, with its full lips, is not the mouth of someone dedicated to prayer. In fact her expression is full of mystery.

(Left) Rogier van der
Weyden, *Portrait of a
Lady*, 1450.

(Right) Diego Velasquez,
Marianna of Austria,
1651.

Public and private faces

A First World War recruiting poster.

The people we are going to look at on the next four pages show the different ways in which a person in a portrait seems either involved with the spectator, or principally interested in his own thoughts. One might think that the difference between a public face and a private one is that in a public face the eyes look directly at you, as though trying to reach you, while the eyes of a private face will be turned away. In fact the eyes of these people are almost all staring straight out of their pictures; but the effect that they make is varied. Here are two public faces.

Getting the message

The bold face on the left was certainly meant to communicate. This is not a portrait; it is a poster, designed in 1915 during the First World War. The man whose face and finger you see is Lord Kitchener, the Commander-in-Chief in Britain, and his message is pretty clear. 'Join your Country's Army!' was addressed to any young man who might happen to pass a wall with the poster on it, and it would be an unusual young man who did not walk on with the feeling that if he did not fight for his country, that terrifying face and finger would go on pointing at him. The way that Kitchener is shown is designed to make a powerful impression: he is boldly drawn, with the lines thick and strong. He is hardly shown as a person, rather as a symbol of the force of duty.

A man of influence

The other painting is a portrait. This is M. Bertin, editor of one of the most important political newspapers in France in the early nineteenth century and a well known figure. Although at this time he was not a young man, he still had the energy of youth. The artist, Ingres, wanted to paint Bertin in as natural a position as possible, and certainly he looks as he must have done in life, with his waistcoat crumpled, and hair ruffled. When you see this painting (it is a large one) it makes a strong impact. The sitter seems to loom out of the portrait, overpowering the spectator with his bulk and the directness of his gaze.

A two-sided face

It is a remarkable face: one side seems to smile ironically, while the other is severe and formidable. There is no attempt to disguise his double chin, but Bertin does not need to be made handsome. Everything in the picture — the way he is sitting, the brown and yellow colouring, the extraordinary hands which appear to echo his facial expression — all contribute to his personality.

Jean-Dominque Ingres, *M. Bertin*, 1832.

These three people are decidedly not interested in the onlooker. The two paintings could hardly be more different, but each tells us a good deal about the characters and feelings of the sitters.

Lady of the sad eyes

The face of Ginevra de' Benci (the juniper tree at the back is a pun on her name – *ginevra* is the Italian for juniper) expresses a strong sense of sadness. We often judge whether people are cheerful or depressed by their mouths: a smile, for example, is an easily recognizable signal. In this portrait, it is not only the mouth which reveals the lady's feelings. Cover the lower part of the face and look at her eyes. You can see that with their brooding gaze and heavy lids they show the same emotion.

She had reason to be upset. In 1480, the date of the painting, she was left by the man she was in love with, the Ambassador from Venice to Florence.

Leonardo

The artist was Leonardo da Vinci, best known for his *Mona Lisa*. You can recognize his work from various clues: the hair, for instance. In his writing, Leonardo compares curls of hair to the swirls of water, and you can see here how he expressed this idea in his painting. Most of all, we can recognize his sitters from the strange, withdrawn look he gives them.

The pioneering spirit

The two other people on this page come from a different society altogether. This is a fairly recent picture. *American Gothic*, the title, refers to the clapboard house behind, and also perhaps to the people themselves — 'gothic' means something medieval, or very old. These are pioneers, from the early days of the United States, who worked hard on the land to make themselves a living. The man's face, with his clear eyes, workmanlike glasses, straight mouth and broad chin, expresses the qualities of old America: determination, courage, honesty.

Look at the pitchfork which the man holds in his fist like a weapon. The shape is repeated more than once: on the dungarees, and even on the roofs of the houses. This is perhaps the artist's way of linking the man to his work and his surroundings.

Any regrets?

The face of the woman is less calm. She stands behind her husband, and looks in a different direction. Her clothes are more decorative, less practical, than her husband's, and her elegant brooch seems out of place. Does she share her husband's convictions, or do the lines round her chin and eyes show she feels differently about her life?

Grant Wood, *American Gothic*, 1930.

Introducing the artist

An artist's view of himself is called a self-portrait. This has always been a popular form of painting — partly because it is convenient, since the model is always available, but also because it allows the painter to study his own character and his changing appearance.

Albrecht Dürer, *Self-portrait*, 1500

A hypnotic face

Here are self-portraits by two famous northern artists. On the left is the German Albrecht Dürer, whose initials you can see in the top left-hand corner of the picture, with the date. It is a haunting picture, difficult to get out of your mind. How has the artist achieved this quality? Partly by the way he has shown his face, staring severely out of the canvas; it is dominated by the eyes, which have a hypnotic strength. The force of this picture does not, though, come only from the features. Look at the way the picture is organized. It gives a good idea of how a face can be made part of a painting's pattern. Dürer's face is placed in the centre of the picture, so that his nose and hand form a central line. His head, from the top down to the hair on his shoulders, makes a regular triangle, with the lower line along the level of his hair.

The artist as Christ

There was a reason why the arrangement of this painting was so important. Dürer, who had a strong religious faith, believed that art should above all be about the life of Christ. In this painting he shows himself, but with the strength and seriousness of Christ.

Taking an honest look

The other painting is by a later artist, Rembrandt. He died in 1669, at the age of sixty-six, and he painted this picture in that year. By this time he was poor and lonely, and his late portraits show his sadness. He seems to be looking into the distance. How is this picture different from Dürer's? First of all, the face is more personal. Dürer overwhelms the spectator: he is not altogether unlike Lord Kitchener (see page 24). Rembrandt does not wish to overwhelm. What his face expresses — through the lines, the tension round the mouth and above all the eyes — is the weight of his long life and sad experience.

Crumbling flesh
In the Dürer, the lines are strong and the details clearly painted throughout. In the other only the face has any importance: many of the outlines are blurred, and we feel that the flesh is crumbling, and almost that we could touch it.

Of course, often an artist will paint himself in a self-confident and cheerful mood, as Rembrandt showed himself as a young man, but many of the best self-portraits are those where the artist has studied his own character and painted what he has seen. Look at Van Gogh's view of himself on p.40.

29

Funny or cruel?

Caricatures

A type of drawing of a person that we often see in newspapers is a caricature. A caricature portrays someone so that he can be recognized, but looks peculiar or funny. Usually the people who are drawn are famous politicians or public figures. Look in a recent newspaper for a caricature of someone who is famous. How friendly do you think the drawing is?

On this page are two pictures of well known figures, which show how this technique works. One of the secrets is to take part of the victim's face which is in real life rather striking (a big nose perhaps) and use that feature as the basis for a drawing of them. Very few of us have regular faces with everything of standard size, and perhaps if you look in the mirror you will find something that is specially you.

The nervous king

Look at the head of Louis-Philippe (once King of France). This is an old caricature, published in a newspaper in 1834. The artist, Daumier, did not like Louis-Philippe at all. He has exaggerated all the King's features, and especially the shape of his head, so that it looks like a pear. (Making a face − or part of one − look like something else is another game played by artists, and there are other examples on pages 14 and 15.) Moreover, three faces grow on one head. Underneath, Daumier explains why he has done this: *Le passé* means the past, *Le présent* is the present and *L'avenir*

the future. The three heads show the King's reaction to different periods of time. How does he react? And what do his reactions tell us about his character?

Honoré Daumier, *Le passé, le présent, l'avenir*, 1834.

I know that face

The other picture is much more modern. It shows a well known writer, Bernard Levin, not looking quite as he would if you met him in the street. He is in the air, kept up by balloons, and the quill pen he holds is bursting one of them. Never mind what those balloons represent; look particularly at his face. The eyes and nose are squashed at the top, and an enormous area of blank face leads to the mouth, much the biggest part of him. Mr Levin writes a great deal, and enjoys making comments and criticisms about other people — so why do you think it is his mouth that is so large?

Of course, although Bernard Levin does not have a face like this, anybody who had seen his photograph in the papers would be able to recognize him. In this case the artist uses details like the hair and the glasses as clues; because a caricature which cannot be recognized has no point.

Gerald Scarfe, *Bernard Levin*, 1970s.

Man and beast

Thomas Rowlandson, *Physiognomical Study*, late 17th century.

The part of an animal that is particularly like a human is its face. We may not enjoy being compared to animals — after all their names are often used to insult people (think of 'cat' or 'cow') — but this fact has not discouraged artists, and some of the most amusing satirical pictures show the likenesses between our faces and those of animals.

Animal farm

Thomas Rowlandson was one of the greatest English caricaturists, with a strong feeling for people's absurdities. Here is a *Physiognomical Study* by him. ('Physiognomy' means the study of a human face, especially its expression and what it reveals about its owner.) The two people are both compared to animals: the woman to a rabbit (does her cap conceal a pair of long, floppy ears?) and the man beside her to a less than attractive dog. The man's nose, the expression in his eyes, his aggressive mouth and even the texture of his skin echo those of his canine companion. Both the man and the dog, we feel, are equally likely to be guarding the front gate of their house with a vicious snarl, while the woman, docile enough but a little stupid, twitches quietly indoors.

The prince and the frog

Grandeville, who did the other drawing, expresses a similar idea rather differently. As you can see, he shows a row of faces. On the left is a perfect profile, in the Greek manner (look at Hermes on page 20): the young man has an almost straight forehead and nose, large, regular eyes, a curving mouth. Six faces to the right he has turned into a frog. The dotted lines are important, and give an almost scientific quality to the drawing. In the first face the line between the bridge of the nose and the centre of the mouth goes from the right downwards to the left; in the second, it is almost (but not quite) straight, and by the time you reach the frog it is quite differently placed. Grandeville is suggesting various things about the face, and about human good looks. A handsome face, he implies, needs to have the centre of the mouth further back than the bridge of the nose (the upper part, between the eyes, through which the line passes). The mouth, too, is very important: the more the lips stick out, the more froglike (in this case) its owner becomes.

Look around you, at your friends or even (if you are careful) your family. Can you see anything that reminds you in the least of an animal?

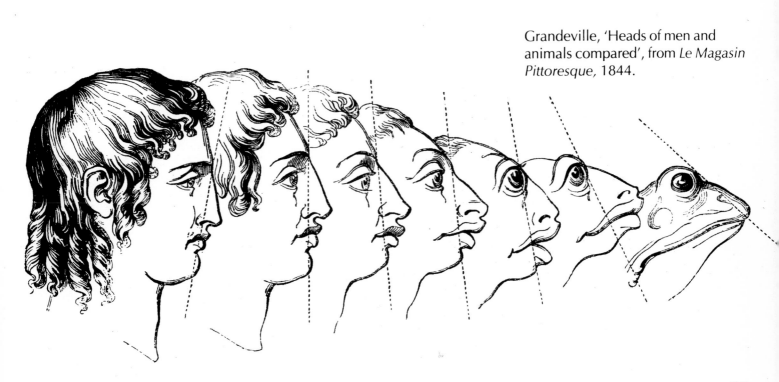

Grandeville, 'Heads of men and animals compared', from *Le Magasin Pittoresque*, 1844.

The faces on these two pages are not attached to ordinary human bodies but, in one case, to the body of an animal and, in the other, to a wooden pole. These two strange carvings come from quite different cultures and are separated by nearly 4,500 years; yet a similar idea lies behind each. The people who made them thought they had special powers. The heads represent respected people who had already died, and it was believed that carvings of them would help the living.

Serene wisdom

On the left is the Great Sphinx, at Giza in Egypt. This creature, carved from solid rock, has the body of a lion and the neck and head of a man. It was built by the Egyptian King Cephren, who lived in about 2500 B.C.; and the pyramid which can be found nearby, 'the pyramid of Cephren', was built as the King's burial place.

The Sphinx's face was intended to represent King Cephren himself. The nose and lips are straight and broad; these strong features were much admired by the ancient Egyptians.

The Sphinx is a monument worthy of a king, not only because of its handsome face, but because of its enormous size. This is much the largest (as well as the oldest) face in the book.

King = god

The Sphinx, and other sphinxes in Egypt, are often confused with the sphinxes in late Greek legends, which are usually female, winged and hostile. But the Great Sphinx is no monster. To the Egyptians who saw it, it must have confirmed the idea that their rulers were all-powerful gods; even today, over 4,000 years after it was built, the Great Sphinx seems as calm, immovable and magnificent as ever.

Kindly spirits

The totem pole also had a godlike power. Poles like this one, carved in wood and brightly coloured, come from North America — ours is from British Columbia, in Canada, and belonged to the Kwakiutl Indians. Totem poles were not simply decorative: they were supposed to contain the spirits of dead members of the tribe, who are shown on them as animals or grotesque humans. It was hoped that these spirits, like King Cephren, would continue to look over and help the tribe. This totem pole was made about one hundred years ago. There are four faces on it: from the top an eagle (with his wings below him), a raven with an extraordinary beak, and underneath that, two human faces. It is hard to tell which is human and which animal.

A typical totem pole from British Columbia, Canada.

The Great Sphinx at Giza in Egypt looms up out of the desert landscape.

Magic, myth and madness

The face without expression

Masks like these and the one on page 12, are especially popular among societies which have not been touched by industrial development. Such masks should not be thought of principally as works of art: as we have already suggested, they have a certain magical quality. If you have ever seen anyone wearing a mask, you will know how strange — and frightening — it is to see a face whose expression never changes,

whatever the person behind it says or does. Here are masks from two parts of the world.

A mask for every occasion

The pair of masks belongs to the Iroquois, one of the tribes of American Indians that lived in the northeastern United States. They were made for a group within the tribe called the False

Masks belonging to the False Face Society of the Iroquois Indians.

Face Society, which was involved in important events in the tribe's life, such as harvest festivals. Each one shows a spirit from legendary history. As you can see, they are surprising. The features are strongly carved, with the mouths and often the eyes highly exaggerated, and they are decorated with

red and black paint. The long, thick hair is real hair — only it comes from horses, not humans. Compared to some we have seen, these masks are not sinister. In fact many are jolly and cheerful.

New shapes for old

The other mask comes from the other side of the world, from New Guinea, north of Australia, and was also used in special ceremonies. The New Guinea example is more formal than the Iroquois, even though it is no closer to ordinary appearances. Parts of the face are treated in an extraordinary way.

Unexpected patterns

The person who made this mask uses the face like a canvas, on which he creates all sorts of unexpected patterns. Look at the triangles around the eyes, for example, or the oval which has been made out of the mouth, surrounded by teeth, with a shape like a dog biscuit in the middle. There is not much humour here; but the effect is very powerful.

A ceremonial mask from New Guinea.

Benvenuto Cellini, *Perseus with the Head of Medusa*, 1545-54.

Medusa – pride before a fall

Perseus was one of the heroes of ancient Greece, and the son of Jupiter, king of the gods. As a young man, he was sent on an expedition to conquer the Medusa. Medusa had once been a beautiful young girl, especially proud of her fine hair. Unfortunately, she dared to compare her beauty to that of Minerva, one of the goddesses. The goddess was so angry that she turned the girl into a monster, with hair of hissing snakes and a face so terrifying that anyone who saw it was turned at once into stone. This monster created confusion and destruction wherever she went.

Perseus and the monster

Perseus, being a hero, was not afraid. He knew that if he saw the face of the monster (it is the face, again, that exercises power) he, too, would turn to stone. He thought of a solution. He approached the goddess while she was asleep, and instead of looking at her directly, was able to see what to do from the reflection in his shield. He cut off her head and that was the end of her. But Medusa's head became very useful to Perseus — it was a sort of secret weapon. He took the head with him, and whenever he was in difficulties he had only to produce it for his enemies to turn into stone on the spot.

Two artists, two Medusas

This story was very popular about five hundred years ago. Here are two heads of Medusa, both dating from the sixteenth century: one a

sculpture, the other a painting. In Cellini's statue we see Perseus just after he has killed the monster: he is holding his sword, and keeping his eyes down so that he cannot see the fatal face. Medusa, here, looks very ugly, but is quite still. In the painting she is shown in torment: round her head the snakes twist and coil, her mouth is open in a scream, and blood pours from what had been her neck.

Both these artists were fascinated by the story of a face that had the power to kill, but they treated it very differently. Cellini's Medusa is in repose, looking as though she were indeed dead. Caravaggio, on the other hand, wants his Medusa's head to be as real as possible, even though it is part of a myth. The

Michelangelo Merisi da Caravaggio, *Medusa,* 1595.

strong lines, the shadows, the bulging eyes, the expression of fear and pain, the masculine look — all give this face an emotional feeling which we might not expect in this subject. Horrible and destructive though she is, we are almost made to feel sorry for this Medusa.

Vincent Van Gogh, *Self-portrait,* 1890.

The tormented artist

Van Gogh's picture, painted in 1890, is a self-portrait. Van Gogh was a man of strange and unstable character; his paintings were too unusual for the people of his own time to accept, although he is now thought of as one of the greatest Western artists. His portrait is ruled, as you would expect, by the face, but everything contributes to the mood.

Look at the way the background is painted, with twisting, boldly coloured, restless lines, even for the coat. The same applies to the head. This is a very tense face and full of violence. The paint is put roughly on to the canvas, giving a feeling of the skin's texture and contributing to the uneasiness of the picture, so that it is difficult to let your eyes lie on any surface. Again, the eyes are especially strong: each seems to stare in a different direction, suggesting the pain, and also the strength, of this man in torment.

Mad and bad

The other portrait shows another madman: not the artist himself, but an *Insane Kidnapper*. It was painted some seventy years earlier than the Van Gogh self-portrait, and in some ways it is less strange to our eyes. The background, for example, is dark and unbroken, and the face does not have the violence of Van Gogh's. But it is an equally remarkable picture. Géricault, who lived in France at the beginning of the nineteenth century, painted this picture as part of a series of insane people, whom he studied in a mental hospital. They included a kleptomaniac (someone who cannot help stealing) and a murderer. They are extraordinary pic-

Theodore Géricault, *Insane Kidnapper*, 1822-3.

tures, especially since they were done at a time when very little was known about mental illness.

The face — mirror of the soul.

Géricault shows a great deal of understanding. This kidnapper, in spite of his gaunt looks, his stare and his odd mouth, is not shown as a monster. It is the eyes that tell us most about him. They are fixed on the distance as though he were longing for something he will never achieve, and as though stealing other people's children was the result not of wickedness but of a need inside himself that he could not fight. The impression that this face leaves — unlike Van Gogh's, with its feverish pain — is one of sadness.

Faces in a crowd

Servants of the household

Sometime in the 1750s, William Hogarth painted this picture of his servants. Six servants may seem a lot for one man but at the time it was quite a small number. The people in this picture are the steward (the chief in the household), the footman, an odd-job boy, the cook (a very important figure) and two maids. You may be able to guess from the picture which is which.

Strong characters

The servants are not shown in a natural setting; in fact it is hard to work out how their bodies fit into the space on the canvas. Nor are they talking together or doing anything; it is their faces that make the painting interesting. There is a resemblance among these faces: the expression (or lack of it), the way the hair is cleared away from the forehead (the men's hair is much longer than the women's), but the picture leaves us with an impression of six individuals. In the end it is the character in a face that makes it worth looking at rather than its prettiness. Hogarth did not believe in making his sitters look more handsome than they really were.

William Hogarth, *Hogarth's Servants,* mid-1750s.

Royal and beautiful

A hundred years or so later Winterhalter, a fashionable and expensive Court artist who did believe in flattering his sitters, painted the children of Queen Victoria. The approach is not like Hogarth's; there is no doubt where all these children are sitting and standing, though we may be less sure which are boys and which girls (at the time, boys were put into dresses until they were about six years old). Of these children, one was to be King of England, another Empress of Germany, and the rest dukes and princesses; would you guess it from looking at them?

Pretty young things?

It is hard to say, more than a hundred years later, whether these children are shown as they actually were; but Winterhalter was inclined in his portraits to paint his sitters as they (or their mothers and fathers) wanted them to look. These children are pretty, but not as interesting as many of the other people we have seen in this book. Young faces are often more pleasant than old ones, but tell us less about their owners. It is possible for young people to have very attractive faces and very nasty characters.

(*Above*) Franz Winterhalter, *The Children of Queen Victoria*, mid-1900s.

The artists in this book

Note: 'c', short for the Latin word *circa*, means 'about', so *c*.1395-*c*.1455 means that an artist was born in about 1395 and died in about 1455.

ARCIMBOLDO, GIUSEPPE (1537-1593) was popular in his own day for his peculiar fantasy pictures, such as *Summer*, page 14, but went out of fashion for many years until he was rediscovered in the twentieth century by explorers of the strange and bizarre, such as Salvador Dali.

BELLINI, GIOVANNI (1430-1516) came from a family of Venetian artists — his relations Jacopo and Gentile were also famous painters. Apart from working on portraits (see *Doge Loredan*, page 10) he also introduced into painting a new interest in landscape, particularly the countryside around Venice.

CARAVAGGIO, MICHELANGELO MERISI DA (1573-1610) had a turbulent life in which he killed at least one man, and was often escaping punishment. He was interested above all in painting scenes as realistically as possible. *Christ at Emmaus* (National Gallery, London) is a characteristic work, and his *Medusa* is in this book on page 39.

CELLINI, BENVENUTO (1500-1571) was most famous as a goldsmith, but also worked as a jeweller and a sculptor. In his boastful and amusing memoirs he made sure he would not be forgotten. His sculpture, *Perseus with the Head of Medusa*, is on page 38.

DALI, SALVADOR (1904-) was always in the news. He once refused to eat a banana in a restaurant because, he said, it looked sad. His pictures, in the 'Surrealist' manner ('surreal' means 'super' or 'more than real') are to be found in many museums, including the Tate Gallery, London and the Museum of Modern Art, New York. His *Apparition of a Face and a Fruit-dish* is on page 15.

DAUMIER, HONORÉ (1808-1879) was an original and expressive painter as well as a political caricaturist (see his cruel drawing of Louis-Philippe on page 30).

DÜRER, ALBRECHT (1471-1528), one of the greatest German artists, is best known for his woodcuts and engravings, such as the series of the *Life of the Virgin*. He was much influenced by his travels in Italy, and by the paintings of Giovanni Bellini. A self-portrait can be seen on page 28.

GÉRICAULT, THEODORE (1791-1824) was a Frenchman who reflected in his work the disturbed period of the Napoleonic Wars. He spent some years in England and was greatly impressed by British artists, particularly Constable and Stubbs. Some of his finest works can be seen in The Louvre, Paris. *Insane Kidnapper* is on page 41.

'GRANDEVILLE' was the working name of Jean Gerard (1803-1847), who was famous in France for his caricatures and illustrations, one of which appears on page 33. The 'Surrealists' were attracted by his work. He died insane.

HOGARTH, WILLIAM (1697-1764), an Englishman, was outstanding not only as a painter in oils (e.g. *Hogarth's Servants*, page 42) but as a caricaturist. His *Rake's Progress* and *Marriage à la Mode* series expressed his satirical view of his own society. The Tate Gallery, London has many of his pictures.

HOLBEIN, HANS (1497-1543) was born in Germany but spent a good deal of time in London. He painted many portraits of the English Court, including Henry VIII and Jane Seymour. His *Edward VI* is on page 16.

INGRES, JEAN-DOMINIQUE (1780-1867) is best remembered for his portraits (one, *M. Bertin*, is on page 25), in which his knowledge of ancient art and of painters such as Holbein helped him create a powerful personal style. One of his finest works is *Mme Moitessier* (National Gallery, London).

LEONARDO DA VINCI (1452-1519) painted *Ginevra de' Benci* on page 26. The *Mona Lisa*, in the Louvre, Paris, is his best known work. He was not only interested in painting: he also made important explorations in the fields of physics, botany, anatomy and warfare.

PICASSO, PABLO (1881-1973) has, more than any other artist of the early twentieth century, transformed the language of painting by cutting up and re-arranging bits of the real world and the space in which they are usually set. His vitality and human feeling led him to explore many aspects of modern life in many different styles. *Woman Weeping* is on page 13.

PISANELLO, ANTONIO (*c.* 1395-*c.* 1455), who painted the *d'Este Princess* on page 8, was an Italian who achieved a reputation for his richly coloured, decorative paintings and the medals he designed.

PRAXITELES (exact dates not known) worked in Athens in the fourth century B.C. and is generally considered to be one of the greatest Greek sculptors. His *Hermes* appears on page 20.

REMBRANDT VAN RIJN (1603-1669) was influenced by the culture of his native Holland, but developed a completely individual style. His portraits include many of his own family and of himself (a self-portrait appears on page 29). Fine examples are to be seen in the Rijksmuseum, Amsterdam.

ROWLANDSON, THOMAS (1756-1827) began by painting serious subjects, but turned to more profitable, jolly pictures of low life and to caricatures in order to pay off vast gambling debts. These pictures present a lively view of England around 1800 (see *Physiognomical Study* on page 32).

SCARFE, GERALD is a successful twentieth-century caricaturist whose work appears in various magazines and newspapers. No public figure is safe from his wicked pen. A likeness of Bernard Levin appears on page 31.

SCROTS, GUILLIM (active *c.*1537-1553), a Dutchman, was Court Painter to the Regent of the Netherlands and from 1546 to 1553 Painter to Henry VIII of England. Pictures of his can be seen in English country houses such as Knole, Kent and Parham, Sussex. He painted the 'anamorphic' picture of Edward VI on page 17.

STUART, GILBERT (1755-1828) was born in America but lived in London for some time where his work was admired. On his return to America he became a leading portraitist. In all he painted some 124 pictures of George Washington — one appears on page 11.

VAN DYCK, SIR ANTHONY (1599-1641) is remembered for his portraits. He was born in Flanders (now Belgium) but produced many paintings in Italy and, after 1632, in England. His pictures can be seen in galleries all over the world and in many English country houses. His *Charles I in Three Positions* is on page 18.

VAN DER WEYDEN, ROGIER (1400-1464) was born in the Netherlands, and was famous in his own lifetime for his austere and penetrating pictures. Only a few survive. *Portrait of a Lady* (page 22) is in the National Gallery, Washington.

VAN GOGH, VINCENT (1853-1890), whose *Self-portrait* appears on page 40, had a difficult and unhappy life and suffered from bouts of madness and suicidal depression. There is a museum devoted to his work in Amsterdam, Holland.

VELASQUEZ, DIEGO (1599-1660), artist of *Marianna of Austria* (page 23), was Court Painter to Philip IV of Spain. *Las Meninas* (see *People at Home* in this series) is one of his best pictures.

WINTERHALTER, FRANZ (1805-1873) born in Germany, was an extremely successful portraitist. He painted smooth, luxurious likenesses of the royal families of his day, including those of England (see *The Children of Queen Victoria*, page 43), France and Austria.

WOOD, GRANT (1892-1942) travelled widely in Europe and was influenced by early German and Flemish artists such as Rogier van der Weyden. He became famous as a painter of American life. His picture *American Gothic* is on page 27.

Finding out more

Books

Most public libraries and school libraries have a section of art books with good colour reproductions on particular artists, periods or styles. Take out those which include artists from this book or others whose work you admire. Apply a critical eye.

Art galleries

It is better, of course, to see the real thing. Go round an art gallery and study a *few* pictures – those which catch your attention or which have been painted by an artist you have read about. If you are interested in portraits, the National Portrait Gallery in London is definitely worth a visit. Art galleries and museums will give information about the pictures in their collections. Some have an Education Officer, and many arrange films and talks on art and artists.

Acknowledgements

The author and publishers gratefully acknowledge those who have lent pictures which appear on the following pages:

Cliche Musées Nationaux, Paris 8, 23, 25, 40; The Post Office 9; courtesy of the Trustees, the National Gallery, London 10; the National Portrait Gallery, Smithsonian Institution, Washington D.C. and the Museum of Fine Arts Boston, Mass. (joint owners) 11; Museum Rietberg, Zürich 12; Roland Penrose Collection, London 13 © SPADEM, Paris 1981; Kunsthistoriches Museum, Vienna 14 and *jacket*; Wadsworth Atheneum, Hartford, Connecticut, the Ella Gallup Sumner and Mary Catlin Sumner Collection 15 © SPADEM, Paris 1981; National Gallery of Art, Washington, Andrew W. Mellon Collection 16, 22; National Gallery of Art, Washington, Ailsa Mellon Bruce Fund 26; courtesy of the National Portrait Gallery, London 17; reproduced by Gracious Permission of Her Majesty the Queen 18, 43; Deutsches Ledermuseum Offenbach/Main 19; The Mansell Collection 20; Dumbarton Oaks, Washington D.C. 21; Imperial War Museum 24; the Art Institute of Chicago 27 © SPADEM, Paris 1981; Alte Pinakothek, Munich (Kunst-Dias Blauel) 28; Mauritzhuis Museum, The Hague 29; Armand Hammer Foundation 30; Gerald Scarfe 31; Courtauld Institute Galleries, London 32; Middle East Photographic Archive – photo A. Duncan; Royal Pavilion, Art Gallery and Museums, Brighton 35; courtesy of Field Museum of Natural History, Chicago, USA 36; and *frontispiece, 37*; Ronald Sheridan's Photo-Library 38, 39; Museum of Fine Arts, Springfield, Mass., the James Philip Gray Collection 41; The Tate Gallery, London 42.

Index